MON ★ SENZO

Written and Illustrated

by

Angela Martin

ISBN: 978-1-0681727-0-0

Do you know what your 5 senses are?

You have:

Two eyes to see which is **SIGHT**

Two ears to listen which is **HEARING**

One nose to **SMELL**

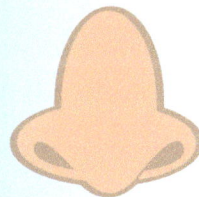

A tongue in your mouth to **TASTE**

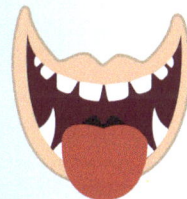

Skin all over your body to **TOUCH**

Sometimes someone can have senses that are over or under sensitive which can affect how they feel and act.

MON ⭐ SENZO is like this and can find some days more difficult than others.

He is also shy and doesn't say very much finding it easier to play alone.

He likes to neatly line up toys.......

.....but on the other hand also likes to make **ALOT** of mess!

MON ⭐ SENZO can repeat the same puzzle over and over again. He also repeats words and phrases.

He likes tossing sand into the air and opening and shutting doors.

He can build a tower block only to knock it down. If another monstar comes to join in and knock it down he will get very upset. He might start throwing toys.

To calm down he may flap his hands or start rocking which is called 'stimming.'

MON ⭐ **SENZO** goes to the Academy for Mon ⭐ z.

It's breaktime and Mon ⭐ Senzo rushes outside to the playground.

"Ahhhhhhh" he calls out and rushes back in to fetch some sunglasses.
It's a sunny day and the light is sore for Senzo's sensitive eyes.

MON ⭐ JOYZ is one of the teachers at the Academy for Mon ⭐ z and wants Senzo to have a friend.

"Senzo we have a new pupil from another country, Joyz says, "would you play with them, they don't speak much English?" Senzo rolls the ball down the pipe and the new Mon ⭐ catches it passing it back to Senzo.

Senzo is feeling too awkward to make eye contact but they both smile whilst sharing the game together.

Back in class later that morning there is suddenly a horrendous ringing noise which just keeps going on and on.

"Everyone make your way to the play-ground" calls out **MON** ⭐ **JOYZ**, "it's the fire alarm, do not run!"

Everyone is led outside where they line up in front of **MON** ⭐ **JOYZ**. Senzo isn't good at lining up as well as loud noises so he becomes very distressed. **"St0000000p!"** he cries out tearfully.

The fire alarm finally stops and Senzo is taken to a quiet room to calm down.

It's lunchtime and Senzo sits down to have crisps, crackers and breadsticks. He likes crunchy beige food but doesn't like sandwiches and alot of other food so has the same snack food every day.

After lunch Senzo gets up to play outside but accidently trips over a school bag on the floor." **Ouch, Ahhhhhh** it's sooooooo sore!" Senzo wails in agony clutching his arm.

"Don't be such a cry baby!" laughs **MON**

RESTLEZ "Senzo has sensitive skin so falling over can hurt alot more than it

would for you Restlez" says **MON**

JOYZ taking a look at Senzo's arm.

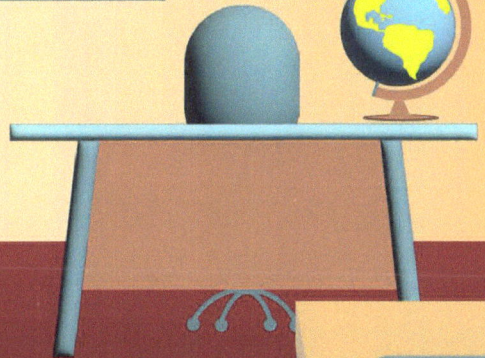

3 + 6 =
5 + 7 =
6 + 8 =
11 + 4 =

Back in class Senzo soon settles down to do some Maths. He liked Maths and is good at it.

" Something has happened to my computer" **MON** ☆ **JOYZ** groans "so I cannot change what's on the white board for you."

"Can I look?" asks Senzo unexpectantly.

"Er...sure" **MON** ☆ **JOYZ** replies not sure whether this is a good idea.

Two minutes later, "You've fixed it Senzo" she beams, "thankyou so much!"

Senzo gives a shy smile and proudly sits back down, he loves anything technical.

3 + 6 = 9
5 + 7 = 12
6 + 8 = 14
11 + 4 = 15

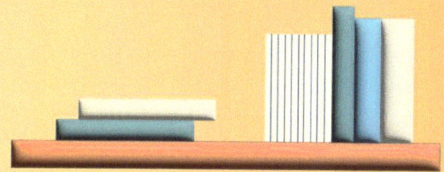

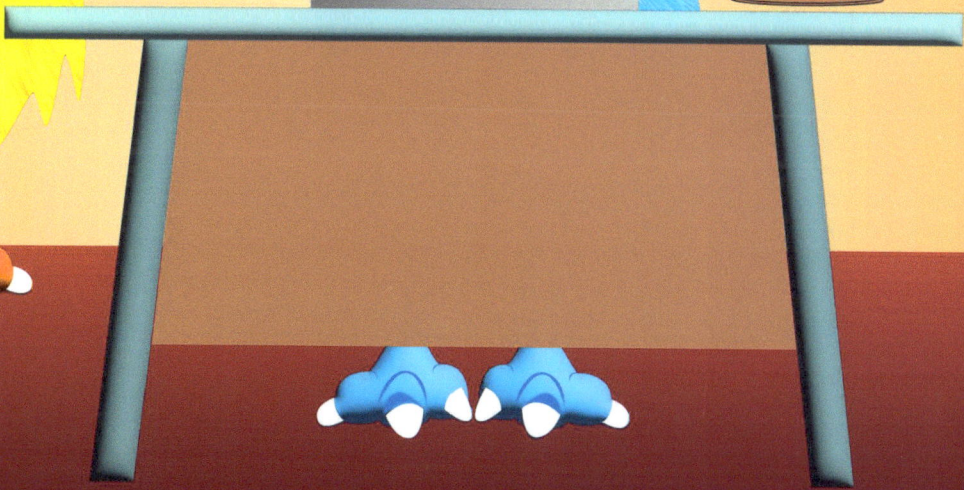

The next day Senzo has to go to the barbers which he really hates. Getting his hair cut is like being pricked with hundreds of needles as his scalp is so sensitive. The barber has cut Senzo's hair before so tries to be as gentle as possible. He also has a tv to watch so Senso is distracted.

That evening Senzo has been invited to a classmates' birthday disco.
Mum had bought him a new shirt but the labels are bothering him so he cuts them off.

He arrives at the disco and the hall looks **AMAZING** with a sky of flashing lights.
Lots of excited kids are running around and kicking balloons. Senzo finds the music very loud and the lights are giving him a sore head. To make matters worse there is suddenly a loud **BANG** followed by a piercing scream, a large balloon has burst!

POP!

It's all too much for Senzo, he has had sensory overload so he flees from the hall and shoots into the toilets.

His heart is racing so he takes afew deep breaths to calm down.

A classmate comes out of one of the cubicles, "You ok Senzo?" he says washing then drying his hands.

Senzo leaps back in shock,

"NOOOOOOOO"

he wails in pain, the hand dryer is

"TOOOOOOOO LOUD!"

The next day is the 5th November and there is going to be a fireworks display at the park. Senzo is scared of the noise so he has no plans to go out that night.
His mum doesn't want him to miss out so has bought him something which could change his life........

...EAR DEFENDERS!

Senzo wears them out to the park that night and loves watching the fireworks.

He doesn't hear the **WOOP WOOPZ**, the **WEEEE WEEEZ** and the **BANG BANGZ** but **THAT** was just fine!

Look who he bumps into too!

FOR MY GORGEOUS BOYS

CORY
DILLON
&
ELLIS

Look out for other books in the future highlighting
non visible disabilities by Angela Martin

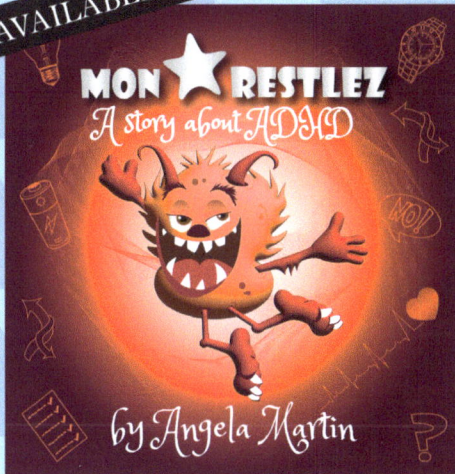

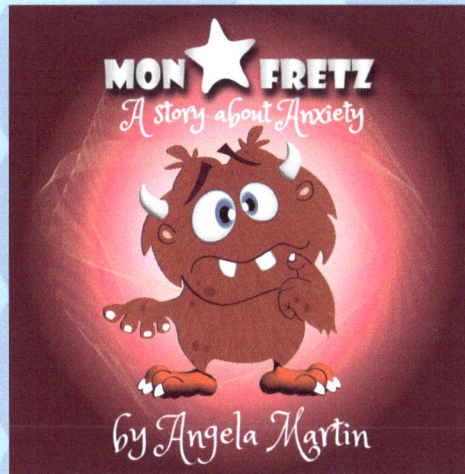

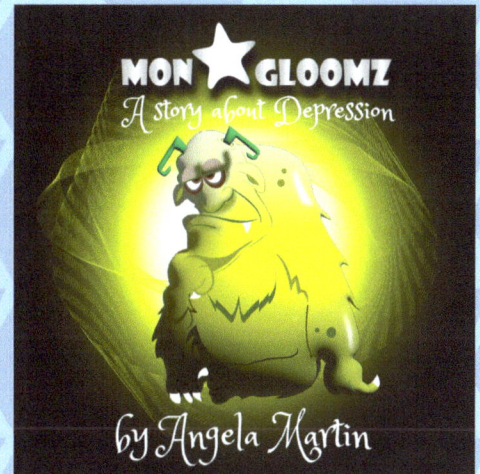

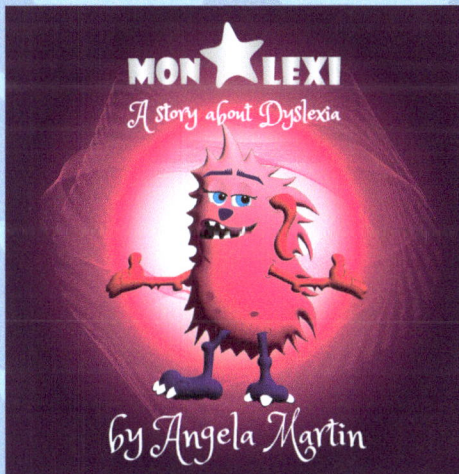

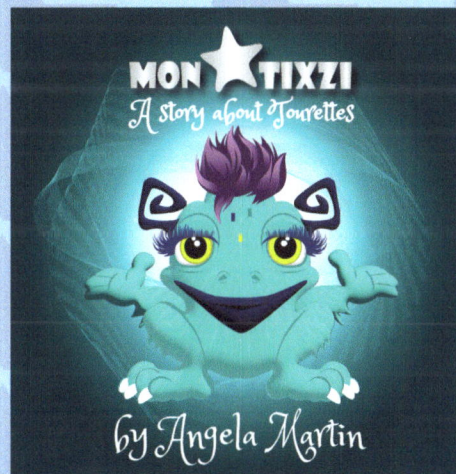

MON ★ RESTLEZ
A story about ADHD
by Angela Martin

MON ★ FRETZ
A story about Anxiety
by Angela Martin

MON ★ GLOOMZ
A story about Depression
by Angela Martin

MON ★ LEXI
A story about Dyslexia
by Angela Martin

MON ★ TIXZI
A story about Tourettes
by Angela Martin

Also coming in the distant future will be books highlighting
obsessive compulsive disorder, dyspraxia and hearing loss.